SMALL CHANGE; HUGE EFFECTION

Empowering the youth generation for America's "fuel" of tomorrow.

JOHN COPPOCK

(All quotes are from John Coppock himself.)

DEDICATION

To my loving mother Retha Coppock for the encouragement. I also want to thank her for supporting me on my journey to success. I was inspired to write this book to help our youth increase their minds, the way they think and view life. To my church family I.C.F.F. overseer Bishop Michael Angelo James, and my immediate church family Healing Clinic Ministries overseer Pastor Love Sr. whom I call my pops because he stepped in as a father figure, especially after my father died, my mom Co- Pastor Tiny Love. To all my family, friends and associates for making this happen, and last because she is the best thing smoking in my life my other half who has always supported me with everything (I love you). Now here is a message to all the parents, do not give up on your child, they are a great gift from God. Everyone is a youth in their own category. Enjoy.

CONTENTS

ACKNOWLEDGMENTS

Special Thanks:
God (allowing this to happen)
Family
My mother Retha Coppock
Bishop Michael Angelo James
Pastor and Co- Pastor Love
Pastor and Co- Pastor McNeal
Healing Clinic Ministries
Kendrick Boykin
Jonathan Holoman
Dr. Howard
Dr. Hart
Professor McMillan
Peers, and finally…..YOU!

CHAPTER 1
OUTSIDE OBSERVATION

As we all know, and if you don't know then you should know. We as people are judged by our first impression, and if this impression if sour so will your reputation be in business. When you have decided to become a business person and become a great asset in it you have to make some small but great impacted changes. One of these changes starts with your attire and manners. The easiest thing about becoming successful in any field of business is the attire. A simple transition from jeans to dress pants, t-shirt to collar shirt and tie, sneakers to dress shoes, jeans jacket to a business blazer, and from sagging pants(only if you do sag) to pants above your waist with the help of a belt. Now I know you might say I have heard all of this before, so since you have then it must be a reason for the theory. I know you have heard this at home, work, the classroom, job interviews, and even exams. This theory is the first great attribute to becoming a success in any form of business. Not only just focusing on the clothing attire, but also you must understand that the style of hair has another great deal of importance when dealing in business. Now do not get mad and aggravated with me about this it is just the rules to this game called business. I know you are like, so how does my hair have anything to do with how I do business? Well think about it this way, have you ever seen a little kid in the store and the parent's hair or clothes look better than their own kids? Well that is the same way in business. Just like parents cannot stand to see a knotty head, or nappy head child, well business people think the same exact way! Business people do not conduct business with half way professional dressed people. If you take a moment to look around you in the world, you will observe that everything has a dress code. All jobs have a dress code but here are just a few to name, jobs such as the postman, police, firefighters, military, and even the White House. Okay let's look at it in another way. Here is a scenario, say a guy is walking down the street with sagging pants, baggy shirt, and a all-black mask on, let's say he walks into the store where you work. What would be your first thought? Exactly! Your first thought would have been that the guy is a robber, am I correct? The funny thing is the guy might just pay for his items and leave, but he may have had the mask on because he might have an unpleasing face that he feared for people to see, maybe something happen to him from a past accident. As on the flip side of that 90% of the time we know it to be a "robber", so we take immediate action; which we should keep doing do not stop that. Anyway there are a lot of different ways you can look at that and also a lot of different scenarios to choose from. So back to the "outside observation", how you are observed from your hair to your shoes dealing with business and not just that in the world period that is how you will be thought of. It is hard and not fair at all but that is just life. Business has rules just as any other thing in life, so if you abide by these rules and tricks to the trades, then you will succeed. Also always remember to keep your hygiene up, you do not want to be in a three hour business meeting with a little stench do you? That would not be a pleasant feeling, nor will it be a pleasant meeting. Well keep reading it gets better. This is only the beginning to the "fuel" for America's tomorrow. In the next chapter I will cover four tips and topics that will increase your "chances" of success in any form of business

CHAPTER 2
THE BUSINESS GREETINGS

Did you enjoy the last chapter? Great it gets better. Now there are some tips that comes after you have understood chapter one. The topics are eye contact, handshakes, speech, and volume. In every business greetings these four attributes are used. You must know the little things to understand their great necessities. When you first meet with people in general whether it is on the professional level or just everyday conversation, the first thing that takes place is eye contact. Immediately following "eye contact" is the handshake. As you implement both of these together make sure that your eye contact is nothing BUT eye contact, combined with a firm handshake. Depending on the gender when dealing with business determines your "handshake" not eye contact but "handshake". If it is a woman you do not shake her hand as firm as a man hands. Give her the proper respect as a woman, and let her know you know the difference between the two. On the other hand women you do not have to focus on firm grips when giving business handshakes. A nice tight grip will do in business. You cannot give a good handshake while looking towards the ground or with wondering eyes. Maintain good eye contact to let the business person know that they have your full attention and that you mean business. Eye contact and handshakes go together just like peanut butter and jelly. Or even as hotdog and bun, hamburger and buns. When you hear or see one, you look forward to the other and when they are not together it seems awkward. Well that is just like business; you cannot give one without the other in "business greetings". After you have processed those methods in your head, the very next thing that comes with business greetings is "speech" and the "volume" of your speech. When I mention speech I mean the vocabulary you speak. No one in any form of business wants to hold a conversation with a person who speaks too low to understand and to loud which is disturbing. Most definitely no one wants to do business with people who speaks slang or well lets be real "ghetto talk". Do not speak the same way you speak to your friends and family, to business people this is very unprofessional. If I greet my family by saying "Yo what's up son?" This will not be the proper vocabulary to use in business. There is a thing called "business vocabulary", and the only way to obtain this vocabulary is through being around people in business. There are different types of vocabulary in every field of business. Eye contact, handshakes, speech, and volume will help you and increase your "chances" of succeeding in any form of business. Remember it is the simplest things that can help our youth or anyone "fuel" in America's tomorrow. Are you still hungry for more?   Well   keep   reading!

CHAPTER 3
A MINDSET "BALANCE"

It takes a mind to make anything possible. Only with the mind will you achieve the impossible. You first have to make up your mind to become a business professional before any steps can be made. The thing that makes taking chances and having open opportunities so powerful is the mind. What can you do without the mind? The mind develops and balances everything, and every decision that we make. Before you wanted to pursue any "goals" you thought about it first. It was not until you made up your mind, that then you proceeded to pursue whatever you thought of pursuing. The mind balances everything from the attire, manners, volume, speech, eye contact, handshakes, networking, friends, goals, chances, distractions, achieving, and even the doubters. Sounds familiar huh? The mind is in control of all these attributes dealing with business. Your mind balances all of these attributes; it also helps you to remember how and when to use these attributes. Business cannot even be discussed if it was not for the mind. Out of all the attributes I have spoken about in chapters one through six, you will need the mind to put all these chapters in to action. I know you might be confused but if you read the whole book and then come back to this chapter you will figure my main point out hopefully. I am going to let you figure it out by yourself because in business sometimes you will have to figure things out alone with little or no point of direction for clues. A mind is a terrible thing to let slip away. With the mind you inhabit leadership. In order to lead you have to follow. To be a great leader, you have to be a great follower of a great leader. Leaders are not made they are born. To be in business you need to strive to be a leader. With leadership skills you develop confidence which attaches itself to your personality. Without confidence this means you have a weak mind, and if you have a weak mind you will not prosper in the world business. Let's go back to the handshakes and eye contact, without confidence you will not be able to perform these attributes correctly. This is why I named the chapter "A mindset balance". I encourage you to read on it gets better. Remember the mind balances everything!

CHAPTER 4
LIFE (TO THE YOUTH)

There is no other way to put this, but in this world you need education. The world revolves around knowledge, so please get some. Do not drop out of school my fellow peers, go to college and get this great education while you can. The more education you have the more options you have to work with. This means the less "money" you loose and the more "money" you make. Everyone wants to make money in business, and education is the key. Business depends on who has the greatest ideas and who is the smartest person for the idea. You can ask any business person that is involved in any form of business and they will tell you to get as much education as possible at least a master's degree. Okay think with me for a moment open up your imaginary cup. Let's say that you have a business and you have just opened. You need someone to keep the books, and keep track of the companies spending. You don't have enough funds to pay someone to do it and your business cannot survive without a book keeper. What do you do? Well if you have a degree such as accounting you could do it yourself and save yourself a ton of money! Trust me education open doors and increases your money triple times. Also remember in the previous chapter I mentioned vocabulary and speech, education will improve both! It will also enhance your business ideas. It is never too late for education. You might believe that you cannot be successful because you dropped out of school, wrong! Go back and get your G.E.D and get into college. You can always get up and try again no matter the age. "Education has no age, just an elevation point". Even in college do not just lock yourself to education think of how you can become successful and what can you do to become successful while in college. Did you know that Facebook, Google, MySpace, and Twitter were started in college? Yes these social networks were created in college. Here is a little food for thought before you move on to the next chapter, Bill Gates, and Warren Buffet was both rich by the age of 23. You can be too!

CHAPTER 5
YOUR "CIRCLE"

My mother always tells me that you are who you hang around. People see you by who you hang around and your dress code. There is an old saying that goes "Birds of a feather flock together". Ever heard of that? Well if you hang around broke people you will be what? Broke! Your "circle" of people that you associate yourself with are your net worth. Be careful who you network with and who you let in your circle of network. When in business you cannot succeed by yourself. Please understand you will always need someone to help you climb to greater heights in business. To have a successful business, you need a successful network or "circle". If you want to succeed not only in business but in anything you do in life, you need to hang around the successful people. It is just like sorting apples or any type of fruit, if you have one bad apple it will spoil the others. So you remove the spoiled one, in order to save the whole batch. This is the same way with business; if you hang around successful business people then you will succeed in business. There is no need to hang with McDonalds workers that do not want more out of life, and you are trying to own McDonalds. Which one sounds better to you, being an employee making minimum wage, or owning the whole business and someone works for you? If you chose being the employee than you should think again. Think about it again, until you understand the theory. You control your own "circle". If you allow negative people to hang around you, soon you will become negative. If you hang around people with a "millionaires" mindset, sooner than later you will adopt the same mindset. Your circle will determine if your business will prosper or fail. Be careful of the company you keep in business, and life in general of that matter. Remember you control your own "circle".

CHAPTER 6
ENTREPRENEURSHIP

Business is a game of chance. That is just how it goes; don't be afraid of "chance". Entrepreneurs are owners of businesses who make money from taking "chances" and "initiatives". This is what you want to strive for, which is to become an entrepreneur. Be your own boss, do not be afraid to work for someone and learn the business way of life, and let someone who knows business show you the ropes to business. In order to be a great business owner you have to follow one. (Chapter 3) Business is not easy no matter what field you are in. everything in life has it risks, but that's what makes life so great, and that what makes businesses successful. Do you remember earlier I stated you cannot have one thing without the other like peanut butter and jelly? Well life and business works hand to hand also. You take things in life and apply it to business to create different ideas, the greatest attribute of business if the power of the question. You might ask what I mean by that statement. I have a task for you, think about what you can provide for the world that can help or increase the need and wants of the people. What do the people want and need? Don't think about the huge things, think small and let it "multiply" to big things. Develop a "mentality" of a business person, which comes with the territory of business you just have to enhance it. Do you have goals? In every aspect of life to achieve anything it starts with a goal. By creating a goal you will increase your focus of direction for your business, this will also increase your network which means more net worth! One thing you have to remember is that creating a successful business will not be a walk in the park. This will be a hard task to fulfill; you will have plenty of distractions. Just do not lose track of your goals or the point of direction that you want your business to proceed. Always ask yourself when you feel down or like you can't push anymore, and even when distractions come ask yourself do I want to be my own boss or be bossed around? Do I want to clock in, or do I want a salary? Do I want someone to cut my check or I cut my own check? All along your journey you will have people who doubt you. These are the main people that will need your services in the near future. Your doubters are your motivation, and your drive. Whatever you believe, that is what will come true. Always speak positive, think, and act positive and you will prosper. Simple manners will take you a long way such as, yes ma'am, no ma'am, yes sir, no sir, please and thank you. At the end of the tunnel called success, the same people who doubted you will be trying to get on board with your bandwagon. "Success is a beautiful thing, but achieving and maintaining it is the struggle". I hope you enjoyed the book, now go out there and succeed! You are never too young nor to old to become successful in business. The question is what can you bring to the table of business? Keep pushing on and be that business person my young people! Everyone is young! Make sure you re-read chapter three to get the overall understanding of the greatest key to your success in business.

Quotes of Inspiration

"Get outside your mind. Change the way you think and we can change the world today. We are empowering the youth generation for America's "fuel" of tomorrow."

"There is no age limit on success, nor is there an age limit in business."

"Change the minds of the youth, then we can change lives."

"Enhance the knowledge of the youth, and we can change the value of a dollar."

John Coppock

"If you help enough people get what they want in life; then you will get what you want in life."   Zig Ziglar

"Start with what you have, and where you are."

Chris Gardner
(The Pursuit of Happyness)

THANK YOU

Thank you for taking out the time to purchase your book and invest in yourself by enhancing your knowledge. Be on the lookout for edition to called Stop Complaining, What's the Solution? Have a blessed day and go out there and succeed! Thank you again!

ABOUT THE AUTHOR

Born on March 7, 1991, John has always been a phenomenal person. John loves to give advice to the youth or anyone who may listen. Now at only 21 years of age John encourages his peers to follow their dreams of becoming entrepreneurs. John officially started his motivational speaking in the year of 2012 at the institution of Benedict College in Columbia, S.C., with the help of the Benedict Staff in the school of HASS. He motivates and challenges everyone to enhance the mind and think different then the common American. Not only is John a great writer, he is a great speaker, and gospel singer as well. John says "I give great thanks to Benedict College, school of HASS, for giving me the opportunity to voice my knowledge to others, without their help it wouldn't have happen."

www.ingramcontent.com/pod-product-compliance
Lightning Source LLC
Chambersburg PA
CBHW021858170526
45157CB00006B/2498